THE CROWNING GLORY™

Fully Rejoice in Being You.

A celebration overflowing with love,
blessings, grace and gratitude. Stand confident within
your truth as your mind begins to serve your heart.

THE CROWNING GLORY COPYRIGHT

Copyright © 2010-2013 by Miranda J. Barrett.
Original Concept Copyright © 2008 by Miranda J. Barrett.
Copyright © 2010 Front Cover Artwork by Helena Nelson-Reed.

All rights reserved. This book may not be reproduced in whole or in part without written permission. In accordance with the U.S. Copyright act of 1976, the scanning, uploading and electronic sharing of any part of this book without permission of the publisher is unlawful piracy and theft of the author's intellectual property.

If you would like to use material from the book (other than for review purposes), prior written permission must be obtained by contacting either the publisher at:

Info@AWomansTruth.com
or the artist at www.HelenaNelsonReed.com
Thank you for the support of the author and the artist's rights.

please note:

The written or spoken information, ideas, procedures and suggestions contained and presented in 'THE CROWNING GLORY' workshops and books are meant for educational purposes only and are not for diagnosis. It should not be used as a substitute for your physician's advice. 'THE CROWNING GLORY' is not therapy and is not intended to replace the recommendations of a licensed health practitioner. It is the responsibility of the reader to consult with their own medical Doctor, Counselor, Therapist or other competent professional regarding any condition before adopting any of the suggestions in this book.

THE CROWNING GLORY™

*Dedicated to the Queen, Goddess
and High Priestess who resides within the
throne of our being and reigns
with a sword of truth
and a compassionate heart.*

MISSION STATEMENT

To guide and facilitate women
in becoming their most beautiful and radiant selves.

To acknowledge and embrace the well of love
and power which lies within all women and to ignite the
awakening and embodying of this life force.

To empower each woman, through exquisite self-care and love,
to live her fullest life possible, and to walk her path of wisdom
and truth, as she shares this light and knowledge
with all beings.

IN DEEP GRATITUDE
Thank you

The creation, birth and life of 'A Woman's Truth' would not have been possible without the love, support and devotion from the following angels in my life:

My beautiful daughter Megan who naturally embodies the teachings of living in her truth and integrity, thank you for the creative gift of the beautiful artwork. Helena Nelson-Reed for her generosity of spirit in allowing her extraordinary artwork, which embodies the teachings so magnificently, to grace the covers. Dennise Marie Keller for her unwavering support and dedication to the teachings and for proofing, editing, aligning and translating my vision into the technical world of manifestation. Dan Fowler for his creative genius and dedication. Lucy Alexander and Suzanne Ryan, my dearest friends for their amazing editing and wholehearted encouragement. Monica Marsh for her commitment, support and belief in the workshops. Maggie Crawford, my mum, for her proofing and for being a living example of the teachings. Cait Myer and Katie Steen for their patience and ability to decipher my handwriting and for formatting the books. Bethany Kelly for her support. Deborah Waring for holding the space for the conception of 'A Woman's Truth' to be born and for her insight in the first year of teaching and Emmanuel for believing in my vision.

My mentors and teachers Rod Stryker, Adyashanti and Alison Armstrong, Max Simon and Jeffrey Van Dyk for their continuous and guiding light in my life, their never-ending belief in my potential and for always teaching me the way to evolve into my highest and most potent self. And to all of you beautiful and courageous women who are committing to living your truth and transforming into your most radiant selves,

thank you.

THE CROWNING GLORY™
Gems of Consciousness

THE CROWNING GLORY 1

I AM…IS THE WAY 5

A COURAGOUS LIFE 9

BEING ON PURPOSE 12

STRESS 14

SEX AND MONEY 19

EMBRACE THE WHOLE 22

AN ACT OF SERVICE 24

YOUR FIRST ACT OF SERVICE 25

UNCONDITIONAL LOVE 27

OPEN TO RECEIVING 29

GIVING THREE ACTS OF KINDNESS 31

BREATH AS THE ULTIMATE TEACHER 33

SUPPORTING RIGHT ACTION 36

LIVE AS YOU DIE 44

TO BE 46

THE FINAL DESTINATION	47
ACTIONS SPEAK LOUDER THAN WORDS	51
CREATING A LIVING MANIFESTO	52
A LIVING MANIFESTO	57
REVEAL MORE TRUTH	58

A DAILY PRACTICE
Commit to Yourself

Commit to yourself. Follow these simple steps daily as a way to instill and strengthen your heartfelt resolve to love yourself. This will help to keep you aligned, transforming and on track, giving you a stable foundation for the rest of your life. As a gift to yourself, please mark the teachings as you read them through and congratulate yourself with each one. See each day as a triumph of your commitment to take exquisite care of yourself.

- ◊ DAY ONE: THE CROWNING GLORY 1
- ◊ DAY TWO: I AM…IS THE WAY 5
- ◊ DAY THREE: A COURAGOUS LIFE 9
- ◊ DAY FOUR: BEING ON PURPOSE 12
- ◊ DAY FIVE: STRESS 14
- ◊ DAY SIX: SEX AND MONEY 19
- ◊ DAY SEVEN: EMBRACE THE WHOLE 22
- ◊ DAY EIGHT: AN ACT OF SERVICE 24
- ◊ DAY NINE: YOUR FIRST ACT OF SERVICE 25
- ◊ DAY TEN: UNCONDITIONAL LOVE 27
- ◊ DAY ELEVEN: OPEN TO RECEIVING 29
- ◊ DAY TWELVE: GIVING THREE ACTS OF KINDNESS 31
- ◊ DAY THRITEEN: BREATH AS THE ULTIMATE TEACHER 33
- ◊ DAY FOURTEEN: SUPPORTING RIGHT ACTION 36

- ◊ DAY FIFTEEN: LIVE AS YOU DIE 44
- ◊ DAY SIXTEEN: TO BE 46
- ◊ DAY SEVENTEEN: THE FINAL DESTINATION 47
- ◊ DAY EIGHTEEN: ACTIONS SPEAK LOUDER THAN WORDS 50
- ◊ DAY NINETEEN: CREATING A LIVING MANIFESTO 52
- ◊ DAY TWENTY: A LIVING MANIFESTO 57
- ◊ DAY TWENTY-ONE: REVEAL MORE TRUTH 58

A LIFE WORTH LIVING

"Never give from your well.
Always give from your overflow."
~ Rumi

All too often as women, your own needs are denied for the benefit of others as you orchestrate your life through demands and expectations you feel responsible for. Unfortunately, this can leave you without the juice and energy needed to be present fully and to enjoy life. During these readings, you will continually discover more about who you truly are and learn the tools needed to live your most authentic and fulfilling life possible. From this place, you will experience being 'full to overflowing' and all the joy and energy this brings.

As you delve into these teachings, you will explore, laugh, study, share, and freely express who you are. In this sacred space, you will ultimately learn your truth as a woman in order to shine, to embody your own beauty, believe in your own worth, and take exquisite care of yourself. For only in this way can you truly be of service.

During these guidebooks, many of the basic needs of women will be explored such as sleep, nutrition, creativity, movement and time to replenish. A topic has been chosen for each book and a cohesive and practical foundation is laid out to inspire and guide you. This will bring about a new strength and resolve which will allow your needs to become a priority, without letting your outer world dictate otherwise. By the end of our time together, the concept of being confident, loving, serene and passionate will no longer be a distant fantasy. Instead, these and many other extraordinary qualities that you naturally embody as a woman will flow with ease, grace and love.

With life's demands so high, it has become imperative that your needs are first acknowledged, honored and then taken care of. From this vantage point, your relationship with yourself then has the potential to be transformed into one of self-love. The beauty is this in turn creates a life that not only fulfills you and your life's purpose, but also allows everyone touched by your presence to receive this gift.

I look forward to spending this precious time with you.

Welcome to A Woman's Truth.

Sincerely and with love,

Miranda

THE CROWNING GLORY

Stand in the greatness of your own supreme magnificence.

Imagine your daily world filled with grace and the essence of grandeur, brilliance and splendor. Now remember you no longer need to visualize this, because you truly do have the knowledge and tools to invoke all these qualities of a glorious life. The meaning of the word glory ignites resplendent beauty and magnificence. Its spirit is one of triumph and great exaltation. This simple word embodies within it a deep sense of honoring and the possibility of you being in wonder of yourself.

This journey of 'A Woman's Truth' has guided and led you down a path of self-discovery. Some of the revelations may have been as simple as needing more sleep each night. Other discoveries may have involved reclaiming your power in an unsustainable situation. The prayer and intention is for you to be filled with new insights and habits, which allow you to shine, be vital and live a life that has a sense of purpose and meaning. It is not about what anyone else thinks of you or even if the masses 'like' what you are doing.

Your Truth is about finding your own signature and dance.
Not the one someone else may have designated for you!

Take this opportunity to acknowledge fully how much you have accomplished during this period of growth and self-realization. As you pause the momentum of time, dwell in this suspension to ask yourself what you have gleaned or implemented during the journey.

Be conscious that to honor yourself fully as a human being you will always continue to grow and change. Yet to see from whence you came and to recognize fully where you are in this process today, will allow you to honor yourself and all that you have fulfilled. This sense of reverence for what you have attained will open up an array of possible pathways for a new and brilliant future.

For change and growth to occur, some basic guidelines will continually support the flow of your life heading in the direction you desire. It is all about consciously pausing throughout your day to check in with yourself to see how **you** truly are. In these moments of listening, you can give yourself what you need to be present in your life and come from a place of self-love while standing strong in your own center.

If it seems as though I am repeating myself, well as the Buddha said, so do the seasons, the moon, the sun and the truth.

"Part of my daily life and heart calling was to connect with my daughter every day, even during the time she was not with me. When she was about to turn eighteen, I consciously chose not to call as often, even though I wanted to. The next day when I saw her, she had a hurt, quizzical look on her face and asked me why I had not phoned. I explained to her that I was trying to let her go. Her response was that she liked my phone calls and could I let go in a different way, please. I was deeply touched. I then realized, as she was getting ready to leave the nest that my checking in with her allowed her to feel loved and cared for. It is no different for yourself."
~ Miranda

In the beginning, this dedication to self-love may have sounded easier said than done. Yet today, with this journey of 'A Woman's Truth' deeply embodied into your soul, you now have a true knowing and relationship with the power of being a woman. The teachings of 'A Woman's Truth' are as simple as building one strong foundation on top of another. As you wove your way through the threads of 'The Grandeur of Sleep', 'Nourishing Nutrition' and 'Embodying Movement', 'The Foundational Trinity' was set in stone.

A completely new level of awareness and expertise regarding self-care has been born. The relationship between your physical well-being and your fear of survival was uncovered. You may have noticed, as you respect and take care of your basic needs, your animalistic nature has become secure, allowing you the space to thrive.

With this foundation, your relationship with caring for your body and your finances was also strengthened. This ultimately led you to living more fully in your authentic feminine power. Coming from this stronghold, all things are possible. As the physical and mental bodies are aligned, are loved, are supported and are nourished, you will stand in your sovereignty and speak your truth naturally.

*"Fill your bowl to the brim and it will spill.
Keep sharpening your knife and it will blunt.
Chase after money and security and your heart will never unclench.
Care about people's approval and you will forever be their prisoner."*
~ Lao Tzu

During this transformational process, the essence of these teachings elevated you into the spiritual realms. This exploration then unified your physical self with your higher spiritual aspects. From this vantage point, your potential is boundless. Now, as you herald 'The Crowning Glory', you are fully embodying your Empress, Queen and Goddess. At this precious moment in time, with all the layers of wisdom aligned and a heightened consciousness regarding what you truthfully need, you can allow yourself to become the shining light that you truly are.

*"There are three methods to gaining wisdom.
The first is reflection, which is the highest.
The second is limitation, which is the easiest.
The third is experience, which is the bitterest."*
~ Confucius

Your only responsibility from this point forth is remembering to actualize what you know and to honor your daily existence. To love yourself is a very untouched idea in this world. Give yourself the accolades and esteem that you deserve. Enjoy and revel in your successes. Override the predetermined and ingrained role of a being a woman, which unconsciously triggers self-sacrifice and the need to be liked.

Make a commitment to take exquisite and beautiful care of yourself, no matter what, and however high this ideal may seem.

Each day you can either allow life to lead you or you can consciously choose to direct your life in such a way that your own values and truths are aligned with your experience. Every one of you has natural gifts and talents. When these are fully expressed and lived, they will produce a ripple effect throughout the world.

Remember, you have endless spiritual power and you are only limited in human form. Therefore, as you invoke the higher realms, your ability to exceed human limitation will be heightened. Consciously choose to be the exquisitely beautiful and powerful woman you are. This is your birthright!

Choose high and live a purposeful life.

'I AM' ... IS THE WAY

Become the prince you have been waiting for.

As you walk this path called life, it is vital to remain elevated above the fears and limitations of the physical world. By being mindful, you will remain conscious that on a higher plain you are genderless and an infinite energy source overseeing your human existence. When humans integrate into physical form they seem to forget this, and become separate from this boundless source of energy. In this disconnect, there is often a silent longing for the unity of 'the one' again. While yearning to make the circle whole, there is a tendency to look outside of yourself for the feeling of completion, a temptation to ask the question or align with another instead of yourself. This results in attaching to being 'of the world', as you become its by-product. Remaining in your authenticity aligns you with your true self as a part of the whole. Then the outer world becomes a by-product of your inner workings.

"Seek information, but not from the unreliable.
Ask for advice, but not from the unwise."
~ The Mahabharata

Become your own wisdom keeper, your own oracle and your own prophet.

Allow this 'I am' to be your guide.

Beyond your story, thoughts, emotions and even your senses, there is a **you** which is calm, still and embodies an all knowing aspect of yourself that is truly who you are. This core being was present before you were born and will remain after you die. This is the immortal energy source that is life itself and from its well of creation, your existence can be orchestrated beautifully. This is only possible if you are not ruled by your mind or emotions. By living from this elevated place, you will naturally be guided, supported and aligned with right action, you will find a sense of peace, and become more conscious and fully alive.

*"The body is mortal,
but she who dwells in the body
is immortal and immeasurable."*
~ The Bhagavad Gita

Remember that you belong to you. Remember that you have the answer to all your questions. Remember that you know the way to follow. And when you are about to fall, remember to fall inward. Do not collapse out into the world or into the wishes and desires of others. When you are broken, in pain or alone, focus on the self. What is it that you need or desire in this moment?

*Whenever you feel abandoned, stop rejecting or abandoning yourself.
Never diminish or put yourself down. See your own achievements
and be supremely proud of who you are.*

SEE WHAT THESE QUESTIONS IGNITE IN YOU:

- How long have you waited to be saved by another?

- How many years have fatal myths of fairy tales lived in your hopes and dreams?

- How can you become your own Knight in Shining Armor? Your own Savior, your own Protector, your own Hero?

- How can you love, honor and respect yourself with such tenacity that the pain of disappointment no longer holds you captive?

- How can you love and love and love yourself again?

Always remember the Real Self knows the way. It is unemotional and unattached to the outcome, even if it is death itself. By its very creed, it is freedom incarnate. The eagle soaring on the wind with a sharp eye on the world below is all seeing, all knowing and witnessing all. This is the Real Divine Conscious Self. Recognize that the human self is but a shadow. Allow your beloved Self to lead and drive the way.

Your 'I am'... is the way.

Take a moment to complete the following statement. Be conscious not to answer this from the limitations of your mind. If you do, it is only capable of painting a very small picture. This question is about evoking the vast expanse of your true nature. Answer the question below from this place, regardless of how wild or unpredictable the response.

Choose words and values that will empower and remind you of who you truly are.

I am...

"I have found over the years three particular 'I am' statements which resonate with my core being, are aligned with my truth and in a miraculous moment, propel me out of fear, victim and limitation. For me at this moment in time, they are 'I am supported...I am love...I am sourced from infinite potential'. I implore you to find your own 'I am' statements that will become daily allies, friends and doorways to miracles. I also thoroughly enjoy sitting in the simple statement of 'I am...' with no attachment to any particular identity and noticing what arises." ~ Miranda

A COURAGOUS LIFE
The quality of spirit that faces danger without flinching.

*I*n times of trouble, what qualities in yourself did you call upon? There are always choices: To cave in and crumble in the face of fear or invoke courage, bringing out the heroine in you to face the challenge ahead.

Without courage, daily threats to your survival can feel overwhelming and become insurmountable. Courage, which comes from the Latin and French word for the heart, invokes the heart forces of love and the qualities of bravery, boldness and fearlessness. This literally heralds images of heroes and heroines!

Therefore, if courage comes from the heart, you will be strengthening this life force through fully loving and forgiving yourself and others. This simple action of love or forgiveness will steady you with the knowledge needed to let your heart lead the way, providing you the strength and fortitude you require.

Now in your life, the chances are you are well acquainted with your heart's desires. You have gained wisdom and understanding of what your physical, mental, emotional and spiritual bodies need. On many levels, you have learned what disheartens you and are hopefully choosing to limit your exposure to whatever dims your light.

This fast-paced world makes it often necessary for you to overexert the intellect and will. Frequently, actions spring forth from the impulses triggered by your thinking mind. At times, this is appropriate, yet if your thoughts continually eclipse your heart's wishes, then you will be living out of balance and not from your center.

It is never too late to become your own heart's desire.

What if you relinquished the belief that courage requires some superhuman force to overcome an obstacle? What if this were only true when it was not coming from your heart? In fact, if it feels like a great struggle or effort, chances are it is emanating from your will. This would be a very different animal indeed.

When true courage is stemming from the heart, it turns itself into an almost supernatural power. The energy is not derived from the outside world. Instead, all the strength and fortitude you need is ignited by the determination that is already alive within you. Courage ignites this bravery and allows it to come from within you. In these instances, you are thriving in the moment. When you stretch out of your comfort zone, poignant vitality and resolve springs to life.

"When I was traveling in Turkey on a motorbike, we were hit by a truck because the driver did not see us. Then to add insult to injury, he did not stop. Miraculously, the damage was not too severe. Yet I was amazed by my reaction. Once I picked myself up off the road, without thinking, I chased the truck. My outrage and courage fuelled my ability to reach the driver's door and pull it open as I roared at the man to stop. I then, literally pulled him out of his cab and dragged him back to the scene of the crime. Police were called, yet it was the look on my partner's face that made me start to laugh. He had such disbelief in what my fearless courage had enabled me to do."
~ Miranda

Many heroic tales are told regarding courage and the ability to overcome insurmountable odds. Where does this power come from? Many would say it is adrenaline and endorphins, which feed these miraculous events. Yet the underlying drive that fuels each one of these situations is a love, either for your own well-being or for that of another. Therefore, it is the force of the heart, which ignites this power.

Let your heart lead the way. Allow valor to abound in your life. Invoke the infinite wisdom of love to guide you. Embody the courage to be your authentic and real self. The more you listen to your heart, the greater the opportunity you will have to relinquish your old ways of fear and become open to the life that is waiting for you.

"Being deeply loved by someone gives you strength,
while loving someone deeply gives you courage."
~ Lao Tzu

BEING ON PURPOSE

Living a purposeful life.

How often have you thrown the insult, 'They did it on purpose?' Meaning, they knew what they were doing and it was not a good idea, yet they did it anyway. You may have also noticed how this statement is often fueled with judgment, criticism and annoyance.

Yet what if 'doing it on purpose' had a completely different meaning. Instead of an insult, it was a compliment. That being 'on purpose' in your life meant the decisions and actions you were choosing to make were deliberate. This is completed with a level of conscious awareness, which supported your ultimate goal of living a full and authentic life. This would certainly elevate you out of the realm of the walking dead.

Purposely living by this code will support you in clearly aligning with your mission statement. Pairing the inquiry to reveal your natural born gifts or talents, together with the power and determination of being on purpose, deeply supports your mission here on earth.

Would this not lead to a more purposeful life?

"Someone once said to me that they had met a woman who was on purpose. The words struck me and kept echoing in my mind. Then, questions started popping up such as: What does it mean to be on purpose? Am I on purpose? As is my nature, I began to inquire. If you are on purpose, does that mean you are being conscious and if so, leading a purposeful life? Is purpose all about being determined and willful? As you can see, it stirred up quite a commotion in my mind. What it left me with was an acknowledgement of my deep desire to live a purposeful life." ~ Miranda

Interestingly, if you are feeling unwell, tired or overwhelmed it is much harder to find the strength and resolve to be courageous or purposeful. Therefore, it is vital to succumb to the inherent wisdom of exquisite self-care, allowing it to be the first line of defense against leading a tepid or unfulfilled life.

HOW TO LIVE A LIFE WITH PURPOSE:

It seems there are two vital components. First, it is about inquiring if you have the health, self-care, courage, strength and determination to fuel the life you desire. This aspect is more about doing and making sure the motivating force behind these actions is aligned with a deep sense of self-love. In translation:

Are you investing enough energy in yourself to fuel your life purpose?

Second, when you know you have the resources to live purposefully, you will then have the vitality and inspiration to unveil and claim the path aligned with your true calling. Therefore, it seems to beg the poignant question:

What is your purpose?

*"Those who have failed to work toward the truth
have missed the purpose of living."
~Buddha*

STRESS
The major player.

*E*vidence suggests that stress is really the ultimate cause of misery and ill health, and that it can tamper with many of the basic, vital functions of the body. When a situation threatens your survival instincts, even if it is merely superficial, the major systems in the body begin to shut down. Unfortunately, the reaction triggered cannot tell the difference between a perceived threat and a real one. In those few minutes of imminent danger, it makes perfect sense for all systems to go on 'red alert' as a way to save your life. As an emergency message is sent from the brain to the rest of the body, blood is redirected away from the internal organs and your immune system and higher intellectual functions are temporarily suspended.

No wonder in times of stress some daft decisions can be made!

When the danger would actually terminate your life, this is a good thing. It gives you the strength and ability to fight or flee the situation. Yet in this present day culture, the world is now full of instances perceived as life threatening. This is where the problem lies. Particularly living in the west when the impetus to achieve and do more is so extreme. This life style has propelled the level of perceived stress to an all time high. Unfortunately, with this overtaxes the immune system and allows disease the opportunity to gain an uninvited entrance. Thus, it is vital to reduce the burden on the immune system in order that it can act appropriately against any real invaders, therefore allowing the body to heal.

The body really is an extraordinary and spectacular instrument and given the opportunity, it will always gravitate towards health and wellness. This is how you are miraculously designed. Yet, if stress goes ignored too long and gets a strong foothold, the immune system's ability to function is jeopardized and the doorway is opened to many an undesirable gatecrasher.

'A Woman's Truth' is ultimately a stress reduction course.

Every angle and suggestion is directed towards reducing stress and balancing your whole well-being on a physical, mental, emotional and spiritual level.

In Miranda's book, 'Nourishing Nutrition', it is encouraged to eat the most important meal of the day which is breakfast and to make sure you do not go for too long without food during the active part of your day. There is a proven point behind this. If you are mindfully fueling your body with healthy food and water, the brain can relax, blood sugar levels remain balanced and the body does not feel starved and will therefore keep the metabolism running smoothly.

When you go for too long without food or liquid, an alert response is set off. The brain can no longer remain in equilibrium as it receives a danger signal. All aspects of your being are under the influence that you are no longer safe. The rollercoaster ride of stress, blood sugar levels plummeting and an overflow of adrenaline all cause a lethal concoction that can ultimately lead to illness.

Those of you who have taken care of a baby, will probably be familiar with the scenario of the non-stop screaming child. 'Well', you think, 'I changed her, she cannot be hungry after all that milk, she is not too cold or too hot. I have cuddled, burped and rocked her. I have made cute, silly faces, sung songs and prayed. What else can I do?'

As you may have noticed, you naturally went through the basic survival needs 'check list'. Would it not be wonderful if you had one of your own? Then if you are still screaming, moody or exhausted after going through your list of needs, you know it must be time to dig a little deeper. As you inquire, you will gain insight into what else might be percolating through your world that is longing for some attention or help. It may have nothing to do with your survival needs, but could be connected to an old cellular memory from the past.

"As a mother, I noticed, when nothing could console my daughter, she was either overtired or getting sick. This may sound quite familiar in your world!" ~ Miranda

To be healthy physically, mentally, emotionally and spiritually, it is vital to manage and reduce your stress levels. The good news is that human nature has an overriding desire to be healthy. What is being brought to light here is the solution.

Reduce Your Stress.

Unfortunately, the unconscious mind does have a mind of its own!

When it comes to weakening the stronghold of stress in your life, a vital component needs to be addressed. Regrettably, many stressful situations can be triggered by unconscious thoughts, beliefs, memories and patterns, which you may not even be aware of. You feel the stress and its strangulating impact, yet you have no idea why you are being so easily triggered.

Imagine in this play called life there is a backstage act also being performed behind the scenes. Even though you are the director, this veiled performance seems to be causing a huge amount of noise and commotion. This unconscious behavior does not allow you to focus on the present moment and seems to knock you off your center. To add insult to injury, many of these unconscious stress triggers are stored as memories in your body's cells; therefore, you have no way of knowing their root causes. Is there a solution you may well ask?

The next time you have guests over and you find yourself stuffing piles into a closet or under a bed, know you are only fooling one of your senses, your eyes. You may be thinking out of sight is out of mind, yet the disarray is still very much alive. Yes you may not see it, but the disorganization still exists.

This is no different to the iceberg below the surface of your mind. Your subconscious and unconscious are much bigger than the little tip believed to be running the show and this influence can become a daunting and stressful component of your life. Yet, with awareness and inquiry, stress will no longer trigger the tension stored in the cells of your body as it has already been released.

Fortunately, there are many ways, which can allow distorted cellular memories to be brought to light and released.

HOW TO FIND, REVEAL AND RELEASE OLD MEMORIES:

◆ **The first step of this journey is to acknowledge that an enormous storehouse of unconscious memories exists.**

◆ **Secondly, realize how this medley of unconscious beliefs, patterns and behaviors may have ruled and dictated many choices and areas of your life.**
This can sometimes be hard to stomach as you see the domino effect of an old fear echoing throughout this lifetime. Yet, instead of falling into judgment and criticism of yourself, allow hope and forgiveness to open up the viewfinder of a completely new world of possibility and choice.

◆ **Then explore and try out different techniques and practices.**
These will become your treasure chests in handling the stress of the unconscious.

◆ **Some profound, tried and tested possibilities are:**

◊ Meditation
◊ Yoga Nidra
◊ Pausing the momentum of life
◊ Less media and technology
◊ Stillness and silence
◊ Time alone
◊ Writing and journaling
◊ Truth letters
◊ Music and movement
◊ Yoga, Thai Chi or any spiritual practice
◊ Time in nature
◊ Doing more of what you love

◆ **These are some amazing books to guide and inspire you through this process:**

  ◊ A Woman's Truth Book Series by Miranda J. Barrett
  ◊ The Design Map by Danielle LaPorte
  ◊ The teachings of Adyashanti
  ◊ Zero Limits by Dr. Joe Vitale
  ◊ The Healing Codes by Alex Lloyd
  ◊ The Four Desires by Rod Stryker

Being mindful and aware that this lurking monster of the unconscious does have a mind of its own, allows you to acknowledge the pink elephant in the corner of your psyche. This empowers you to tame the wild beast, reduce its impact and live your life more front stage and center.

what is your own personal stress reduction 'check list'?

*"Holding on to anger is like grasping a hot coal
with the intention of throwing it at someone else
— you are the one who gets burned."*
~ Buddha

SEX AND MONEY

The leading roles in the game of stress.

A whole segment of 'A Woman's Truth' is dedicated to the world of money. This is not a mistake! If you wish, you could think of the time well spent as a charitable donation to your well-being. It is next to impossible to remain relaxed, happy and carefree knowing you do not have enough resources to cover your own and loved ones basic survival needs.

Therefore, if your world of money is still topsy-turvy, with too much cash spewing out and not enough pouring in, pay attention! As discussed in the 'Abundance of Wealth', your relationship with money can be a poignant tell, just as in a good game of poker. If your poker face of 'everything is fine' is no longer working, then you need to wake up and become conscious enough to know if you are taking yourself for a ride. Is the money situation in front of you desperately in need of some fine-tuning or are you laughing all the way to the bank?

When it comes to intimate relationships, money is a major cause of commotion. How often in your life has some discussion over finances become fraught, emotional and overwhelming? Often it seems that the issue in question is being attacked from both angles. There is your perception and beliefs about how the money should be spent, saved or squandered. Then there is also the opinion of the other person! In any partnership, if the dynamic of money is not openly discussed, negotiated and agreed upon, the relationship may ultimately fail.

You are not alone if this sounds familiar.

Everyone has their own turmoil and distorted beliefs around money inherited from their culture, ancestors, family and experiences. If you cannot find common ground and a unified sense of purpose and value surrounding the charged and volatile energy of money, it will be challenging to find tranquility within this world of currency.

"I have certainly had first-hand experience in this dynamic of making emotional decisions surrounding money. When I believed love would conquer all, I had a tendency to be overly loyal to my partners. My rather prejudiced view of their potential often led to over investing in their lives and not enough in my own. This would lead to feelings of both betrayal and resentment in my world of money and relationships. I am grateful, I am now at a point in my life where I hope and pray that I have become an expert due to the many and outrageous mistakes I have made." ~ Miranda

Unfortunately, sex is not that much different. A woman's sexuality can be used as a tool, sold as a commodity and is certainly a powerful bargaining chip. How often has this sacred part of your femininity been exchanged, abused, disrespected or given away? The deepest crime it is to whom are selling your sacred feminine.

As you walk this path reclaiming the infinite power of the feminine that resides within you, the beauty is you will never again feel the need to give yourself away. When you acknowledge, honor and recognize your sexuality as sacred, and are living in the very depths of your feminine heart, you will naturally guard her with your life.

Never Again Does Anyone Enter Your Realm Uninvited.

only the honorable and respectful are allowed.
only those who treasure and revere who you are called upon.
only the worthy who affirm the divinity of your feminine power are invited.
only those who recognize the honor, grace and privilege
of entering your sacred being;
only they are welcome.

The journey of falling in love with yourself parallels whom you allow into your intimate, sacred circle of being. In the sanctified union of sexuality, you are at your most vulnerable and open. You are absolutely at the mercy of the deep well of your emotions, which reside within you as a woman. By knowing that you are about to reveal and unravel your layers of protection, does it not seem imperative for you to know that this person deeply loves you and would die for you?

"When my daughter was turning of an age where boys and sexuality were becoming highly appealing, I told her the following: I would encourage you to not be sexual with any man unless you know he would willingly die for you. If you know this, you also know that he will love, honor and protect you in the sacred and vulnerable act of lovemaking. I wish someone had told me this during my wild and rather unabashed exploration of my sexuality." ~ Miranda

A rather horrifying thought in this realm of sex, is that every time you are intimate with someone, you are also sharing with every partner they have been sexual with. Obviously, this is not always a good or happy ending! Therefore, choosing to be selective and discerning about whom you are intimate with can become a declaration of love for yourself, your health and your overall sense of well-being.

"One of my biggest lessons regarding sex was the idea to slow it down. I have never had a one-night stand, as it is not in my nature. Yet, I found if I gave in to being sexual too fast, I felt as though I was on a fast track of intimacy without a foundation. In reality, I do not know this human being on any other level apart from his physical body. I personally have a three-month rule where I am not sexual with another person during this time. It then becomes outrageously clear if he is just after sex, which is certainly not my agenda. I then get to know who he is on many different levels and to figure out whether he would die for me before I choose to share the most intimate part of my being with him. I have offered this concept about the three-month rule to many of my clients. They say they hear my voice in their head, often with an English accent, which I find hilarious. Yet sometimes they choose to ignore me. In the morning or days after, it is often apparent why waiting may have been right action." ~ Miranda

This topic leads beautifully to the following discussion on embracing any mistakes you may have made. How many of you regret some past scenario that involved either sex or money?

EMBRACE THE WHOLE
Mistakes and all.

To become an expert of your life, many mistakes will be made and many lessons learned. This is the journey of becoming a connoisseur of you.

What would happen if you embraced your failures, mistakes and limitations? It is a novel idea. Know that by claiming all your strengths and weaknesses, power and insecurities, loving-kindness and resentful hurts, you can then become whole and fall madly and deeply in love with all of who you are. By unveiling the spectrum of the rainbow that lies in the depth of your being, you have the ability to open and reveal all of your power, your truths, your light, your dark, your shadow and your spirit. What a glorious image!

"At this point in my life, I am acutely aware of my strengths and weaknesses. Directions, technology and paperwork are definitely my downfalls. Yet creativity, spirituality and guidance are certainly my strengths. For years, I gave myself a hard time for being inefficient at running the technical or linear side of my business. Now I know better. My new strength is to choose not to waste my time or energy on this aspect of my business and instead, I invest my money to pay brilliant people who are technically strong. They are like my angels in linear human form!" ~ Miranda

Therefore, the next time you screw up; notice how your default switch reacts. Is it with forgiveness and loving-kindness or with judgment, harshness and criticism? Remember, there is always psycho bitch living in your head ready to jump on any tiny digression or mistake. You may not be able to control her first banshee wail but you can certainly empower yourself by choosing to turn down her volume and tuning back in to your compassionate loving heart. You may well have an imprint from childhood fueling the judge and condemner.

Is this critic who you are choosing to be today?

With the knowledge that 'A Woman's Truth' is all about falling in love with you, it seems appropriate that you treat yourself as you would a young child who you adore.

"A young girl was staying with me. She was a beautiful, sweet being. She accidentally dropped a glass that shattered into millions of pieces on my tiled kitchen floor. My concern was for her bare feet. She put on her welly boots and we cleared it up together. As she apologized profusely, I watched her face. I could see that she must have been seriously reprimanded in the past for such an accident. I continually reassured her and made it a game to find the shiny shards of glass. Yet it broke my heart to see the impact on her. I really could not care about the glass. I was more concerned with her broken confidence." ~ Miranda

Take a moment to ponder someone you respect and who is an expert in their field. The chances are they have been at it for some time. If you asked them about their experience, they would probably have tale after tale of horror stories, which have had an impact on their successes and who they are today. Becoming a mistress of any trade is through trial, error, triumphs, failures, sheer luck, perseverance, keeping your wits about you and keeping a sense of humor.

As human beings, we learn through our mistakes.
The wisdom and sanity is in not repeating them repeatedly.

AN ACT OF SERVICE

Being truly of service.

It may be easier to discern what is not an act of service. It has nothing to do with 'should' or 'should not'. In fact, judgment will defy any act of kindness. You will not find one on a 'to-do' list and it certainly will not be an act forced upon you. The generosity of any gift given from the heart is greatly diminished if motivated by anger or resentment.

In fact, it seems as though a pure act of service comes from the heart where it is fueled by love, care or desire. It can sometimes have an impulsive, playful or even spontaneous energy. Yet undoubtedly, its origin comes from the heart forces and is intended to be of help or service.

Yet, beware of the pitfalls. You have probably fully realized by now how women tend to give of themselves even when they do not have the energy to do so. Problems arise when the heart is leading you to say yes, but the body does not have the reserve, energy or juice to accomplish the goal. It then becomes detrimental for you to bulldoze through the situation anyway.

The beauty of a true 'Act of Service' is that the giver and the receiver win. Imagine what an impact True Service would have on the world and your community if this concept were fully embraced. The ripple effect of everyone aligning with self-care and then coming from this strong power source and well-being would literally be priceless!

"There have been occasions when something has been asked of me and everything in my being wanted to participate and give the gift of my time, money or energy. Even though there may have been a resounding intuitive yes, I have found it vital to discern if my physical body has the time, energy and resources to fulfill the request before I respond aloud. By choosing to pause the momentum, particularly when my plate is already full, I can then consciously decide not to overwhelm myself. This is when the power of being able to authentically say no without any guilt is invaluable." ~ Miranda

YOUR FIRST ACT OF SERVICE

"The first love affair is always with the Self."
~ Rumi

Does your life feel full to overflowing in a good way? If not, then this is your first priority and act of service, to replenish, nourish and align with yourself. Then you will actually have something to give.

Have you ever noticed how your energy levels affect your ability to provide? When you are tired, the effort of going the extra mile can seem overwhelming and literally as though you do not have it in you. Yet, when you are replenished and rested and someone asks a favor, your heart forces naturally respond with a resounding yes.

"I often wonder how life would be if we could only love ourselves as we love someone in the first few months of a romance. If we poured that much love, consideration, attention and time into ourselves, my sense is the result would be quite glorious. We would glow, shine and certainly be full to overflowing. Therefore, instead of this being an 'if only' scenario, make it a reality by consciously falling madly and deeply in love with yourself as your first act of service." ~ Miranda

*"I wondered why somebody didn't do something.
Then I realized, I am somebody."*
~ Author Unknown

PONDER YOUR POSITION ON LIFE'S TOTEM POLE:

◆ Are there priorities that are eclipsing your well-being?

◆ **Who or what is more important than you are at this juncture in your life?** If you are not number one, put yourself in first place in big letters now. Practice makes perfect!

UNCONDITIONAL LOVE

Living between the lines of your conditioning.

As you become less and less judgmental of yourself, you will naturally fall in love with all of your aspects, the good and the bad. This will also result in you becoming less critical of others and is literally a win-win situation. It seems the one quality this world certainly needs more of is an infusion of unconditional, untainted, pure and unadulterated love.

In 'Speaking Your Truth', the concept was introduced that everyone has their own personal perspective. Even if their viewfinder is completely different to yours, this does not necessarily mean they are wrong. When you become aligned with your truth and stand in your own power, you are no longer dependent on having to agree with others or desperately wanting them to concur with you. Your truth holds its own, yet it does not become a dictatorship. From this standpoint:

The opposite of a truth is another truth.

By remembering the possibility that many different truths can co-exist in harmony, you fighting for your way or the highway will loosen some of their grip. This will release the stress and tension inside and allow others to exist and possibly flourish or diminish in their own circle of truth. By releasing the impulse to change their mind for them, you can then return to yourself. This allows time to discern your loving right action and send whoever is causing you grief buckets of love and prayers on their journey, however crazy it may seem! Remember you do not have to agree with their point of view and you certainly do not have to follow their way if it is out of your alignment. This also does not mean you have to stop loving them.

Love in and of itself has no agenda or opinion.

Therefore, when you stand in the arms of unconditional love, you are allowing yourself and others to be themselves without trying to distort their essence to gain love. In this realm of unconditional love, you are ultimately free to be yourself and are giving others the same gift of true liberation. This precious gesture can only be born of the heart, therefore it is imperative to send love, compassion and non-judgment to your own ego, as she is the one who will fight and defy the very concept of absolute love. The ego's survival attracts all its power and might from its essence of being opinionated, separate and proving herself to be right, thus eliminating the possibility and concept of receiving the boundless love of another.

*"If your compassion
does not include yourself,
it is incomplete."*
~ Buddha

OPEN TO RECEIVING

For what you are about to receive...

The concept of receiving is a vital part of being a woman and fully claiming your feminine power. In many traditions, the left side of the body pertains to the feminine and the ability to accept the gifts life lavishes upon you. The left knee often corresponds to the energy of the mother. If you notice you are having physical symptoms on your left side, it may be in connection with either giving too much or not being an open vessel to receive.

There are always two sides to any situation, light and shade. Yes, it may sound like a genius plan to be an open and porous vessel to receive. However if what is barreling towards you is a train wreck of negative emotions, obviously this is not conducive to your well-being. It is all about balance, discernment and self-care.

POTENT AND HEALTHY WAYS TO RECEIVE:

◆ **First and foremost, give loving acts of kindness to yourself daily.**
Then your own tank will be full to overflowing and you will be able to discern if it is right action to let something or someone into your energy field.

◆ **Take superb care of your 'Foundational Trinity' of sleep, nutrition and movement.**

◆ **Speak your truth and say yes and no as appropriate.**

◆ **Reduce and eliminate stressful habits, people and events from your life.**
"It is a well-known fact that I do not do malls!" ~ Miranda

- Fill your life with playful endeavors and people who replenish your well.

- Once you are in your center and balanced, you will become acutely aware if what you are about to receive is love or a dagger in disguise.

Remember the pause button.

Often, old patterns and learned behaviors will trigger a present day situation. By taking a moment and a couple of deep breaths, you can pause long enough to remember that you know how to take care of yourself and therefore will consciously choose to act in a way that is beneficial for you. The other option is that there is no choice and you react as if a stick of dynamite lit all the way back to your childhood.

"There are certain situations that still trigger me. I hope this will not be true to my dying day. My biggest shift is that now I choose to be compassionate with myself when I am provoked. I am certainly less reactive than I used to be!" ~ Miranda

By remaining in your center, well fed, rested and exercised, the chances are you will know the difference between receiving a hug or a punch! As you wade through your day, pay attention to the messages of your body and to the many opportunities for help that constantly surround you. The bottom line is that you actually need to pause long enough to receive whatever is available or is being offered in your energy field, whether it is a smile, a helping hand or an actual gift. In this ebb and flow of giving and receiving, be mindful to keep the balance.

- Just as you choose to give 'Three Loving Acts of Kindness' to yourself each day, choose to receive three as well.

- Then from this overflowing well, you will have plenty of energy to give to others and truly be of service.

This waxing and waning of giving and receiving
will naturally keep you beautifully in your center.

GIVING THREE ACTS OF KINDNESS

Giving is receiving.

All that is required is performing three acts of kindness a day. It can be as small as letting someone cross the road or giving a dollar to a homeless person. You will notice it takes very little energy to be kind and loving. A smile can replace a glare, a thank you instead of silence as someone holds a door open. Literally, these little acts of benevolence change the tide and cause a ripple effect into the world. By consciously choosing to do three loving acts of kindness a day, it will inspire moments where you will rise up from your animal instincts and decide to tread the higher road with a loving and kindhearted gesture. The added bonuses are that both parties leave the moment feeling full and cared for. It takes a lot of work and suppressed energy to remain angry and resentful for too long.

"I have to say that many of my kind moments are used while driving around Los Angeles or with my beautiful teenager. It is so easy to want to swear at the 'idiot' who is talking on the cell phone instead of paying attention to the road. Instead, I take a breath, remember my decision to act with kindness and give them the room to maneuver out of the situation. I might even smile. Instead of becoming angry, I bathe myself in compassion. This certainly saves my stress levels and I tend not to carry the situation with me once it is over." ~ Miranda

It is vital that you only choose to give acts of kindness if you have already invested in yourself and your well is full. Sometimes it is instinctual to lend a helping hand, yet if you have no energy to give, realize you are not truly being of service as you are jeopardizing yourself.

Once you are naturally taking exquisite care of yourself, giving from your overflow will lighten and lift your spirits, rather than dampen your smile.

A genuine smile is an ultimate gift of kindness.

PROVIDING THREE ACTS OF KINDNESS A DAY:

- ◆ **Consciously commit to bestowing three acts of kindness during your day.**

- ◆ **Some days you may choose to use more than three. This is all good karma!**

- ◆ **Throughout your day, notice these acts.**
  You may even seek them out. It could be as simple as picking up someone else's socks or offering a glass of water.

- ◆ **Notice how these acts impact you.**

How does performing a simple act of kindness make you feel?

Eventually, what happens is that living from a loving heart becomes the norm. This includes how you treat yourself above all else, which will then be reflected in how you treat others.

"The best memory is that which forgets nothing but injuries.
Write kindness in marble and write injuries in the dust."
~ Persian Proverb

THE ULTIMATE TEACHER BREATHES

To give, to pause and to receive.

Breathing is a miraculous gift of life. You do not even have to think about breathing, it just automatically happens. It may change its tempo now and then, but while you are alive, it comes and goes like the tides and the moon. It is a simple and powerful expression of being alive.

Interestingly, the breath beautifully mirrors how to behave in the world. You breathe in and receive oxygen and life force. You breathe out to give space to breathe in again. Without this process, you will die and quickly at that. You can live without sun, food or even water for short periods of time, yet without breathing, you will depart this life rapidly. A flow is exquisitely ordained.

We breathe in ~ we breathe out
We receive ~ we give
We replenish ~ we release
We inhale ~ we exhale
We collect ~ we give away
We expand ~ we contract
We ebb ~ we flow
We wax ~ we wane
We inspire ~ we expire

◆ Take a moment to sit and watch your breath.

◆ Notice is your inhale or exhale stronger?

◆ Now see how it feels to lengthen your exhale and keep breathing out.

At first, it may calm you and even draw your attention inward, yet after a moment you may feel as though you are literally suffocating or deflating. Then a primal instinct will engage to change the decision and force you to breathe in.

In translation, you are required to receive.

This is a poignant analogy for life. The body is designed so that you are unable to hold your breath for too long. The autonomic nervous system will take over and you will instinctively gasp for air. Yet when it comes to your life, you may sometimes spend days, weeks or months in a symbolic exhale. Giving... giving... giving. Yes, you will eventually collapse, often through illness, which is the body's way of saying that you must stop, breathe in and rebalance your life.

"In my work, I often notice when my client is touching on a deep, old emotional wound or reliving a stressful moment. Their breath becomes shallow and practically nonexistent. Unfortunately, for me as an empath, I feel this in my own body and will ask them to breathe for both our sakes. Unaware of their suffocation, they will often inhale deeply and we can both move forward with the knowledge that we are not going to expire through lack of air." ~ Miranda

You breathe in, you breathe out. It is a beautiful and rhythmical dance of energies.

How are you living this dance in your life?

Are you giving and receiving or are you just giving, giving, giving?

Sometimes to rebalance, the inhale of receiving might need to be longer than the exhale of giving or vice versa. Think of nine hours of undisturbed sleep or a pajama day as one long inhale that will address a week of long exhales. Become conscious of continually readdressing the balance.

Your relationship with the rhythm of your breath will teach and show you if you are centered. If you notice your inhale is shallow, it is time to pause, slow down and receive. It could be as simple as taking a few minutes standing in the sun and dropping your breath deep down into your belly. If the exhale is shallow, it is a sign that you are in stress mode and are certainly not full to overflowing.

The simple act of taking a few deep breaths will bring you back to the relaxed part of the nervous system. It will literally return you back to your center and from this place of equilibrium, you will have the power and insight to discern whether giving, receiving or being still is the right action.

The pause.

The pause between the breaths can actually be one of the most precious moments in life. You are neither giving nor receiving. In fact, you are in a state of stillness and if you choose, possible grace.

Sometimes not acting is the right action because it allows you to become still, silent and regroup. Obviously, in the world of breath, this pause cannot last too long, yet in the world of your choices this stillness is always a third option.

There are three choices in life: To give, to receive or to be still.

As the expression goes:

"Be still and know that I am God."

This can also be translated as:

Be still and truly know yourself.

SUPPORTING RIGHT ACTION
creating the life you truly desire.

The concept of right action is a fundamental and stabilizing practice for life. When you pause for a moment to identify the correct path, the insight you gain will have a powerful influence on what you ultimately choose. This sincere inquiry can function on many levels and layers of who you are.

Put simply, laws are often established as a path to right action. They are based upon the idea of providing guidelines, which help people to live a more peaceful life. Imagine driving a car without any laws in place. The chances of surviving until you reach your destination would be slim. Driving is best accomplished when everyone on the road obeys the same rules maintaining a sense of order and survival.

Within your own life, there are certain laws or truths about yourself that also need to be honored in order for you to maintain a sense of peace and well-being. "A Woman's Truth" is all about discovering these truths within you and placing them in alignment with the rhythm of your life. Sleep is a perfect example of this. For some, functioning without at least eight to nine hours of sleep every night causes mayhem. Yet others find it right action to sleep only seven hours. This is determined by each individual's truth and life style. There is no right or wrong. It is all about finding what benefits you the most.

"One night I was invited to a fundraiser. It sounded fun and was at a store I love. But as my day progressed, I felt that I had less and less energy and the idea of going out again no longer held such appeal. Yet, there was this voice nudging me to go. I knew an old friend was going to be there and I wanted to connect. However, my dedication to taking care of myself, which would mean staying home, was also calling. What a quandary. Yet over the years, I have learned to listen to my intuitive Self. It had no agenda, yet was clear in its direction. 'Go to the fundraiser.' So I did. During the time I spent there, I made three auspicious business connections, including the storekeeper, who agreed to sell my book. As I drove home, with a full moon in the sky, I smiled to myself. I was grateful that I had listened and was energized by the conversations and potential opportunities. Obviously, it was right action to go." ~ Miranda

Sometimes right action may not make any sense to you at the time, yet there is a gnawing feeling that it would be highly beneficial to behave in a certain way, even though the reason itself may elude you. Hindsight is a wonderful thing, yet where would all the adventure be if you always knew the exact outcome?

In your past, there may have been times when your behavior was uncharacteristic, yet in the situation it was perfectly appropriate. When you answer to your Higher Calling or make a decision coming from your intuition, you may well find yourself performing tasks or taking actions that only make sense to you or others later.

Meditating or holding space for right action can open many doorways and possibilities for you. This silent listening allows for a new sense of grace and flow to enter into your life.

Before you even begin to go through this checklist, take a few deep breaths and drop your attention down into the belly. This will connect your mind back up to your body. If you respond only from your head, your inner bitch and judge might have some very strong opinions about how you are not doing any of this perfectly. Yet if you come from your heart, you will invoke compassion for yourself and you will see clearly that you have made astonishing leaps and bounds in the right direction. This is a time to celebrate all you have already become and for you to bring awareness to areas that may need some attention.

"I know you're tired but come, this is the way."
~ Rumi

Please lovingly remember, this is a journey, a learning curve and we all have a lifetime to fall down, pick ourselves up, get lost in old behaviors and then find ourselves again in the present moment. There is no perfectionism in life. All that perfectionism will suffocate the yearning in you to transform because it believes you have to be perfect before change can occur.

"In my own life I have become acutely aware that if I allow my perfectionist to rule, many projects are delayed in their launch. I tend to delve into the potential situation mainly with my mind. In addition, of course, like a dog digging for a bone many aspects are unearthed which are far from perfect. Unfortunately, this cycle stops the flow of inspiration and creativity, leaving me stuck in the world of nitpicking details and fixing flaws. Not a realm I desire to live in as it is filled with judgment and criticism. To be honest, it is a very bitchy tone of voice!" ~ Miranda

WHERE ARE YOU ALREADY LIVING IN RIGHT ACTION?

Choose to amplify any positive behaviors daily. If a certain behavior is not being lived, honor it by inviting it into your life allowing it to become a habit.

Your Physical Life:

- ◊ Getting enough sleep, rest and down time
- ◊ Consciously unwinding before bed
- ◊ Eating breakfast
- ◊ Drinking plenty of water
- ◊ Eating nutritious life-giving foods on a regular basis
- ◊ Moving the body daily on a regular basis
- ◊ Practicing Kegals daily
- ◊ Finding an exercise you love
- ◊ Breaking a sweat often
- ◊ Taking care of your body as a temple
- ◊ Embodying your sensuality and sexuality
- ◊ Listening to the body's messages and taking the appropriate actions
- ◊ Becoming more conscious to breathe fully throughout your day
- ◊ Using the breath as a powerful tool to calm you when you feel stressed
- ◊ Inviting in loving physical contact, hugs count!

"This being human is a guest house.
Every morning is a new arrival.
A joy, a depression, a meanness,
some momentary awareness comes as an unexpected visitor...
Welcome and entertain them all.
Treat each guest honorably.
The dark thought, the shame, the malice,
meet them at the door laughing, and invite them in.
Be grateful for whoever comes, because each has
been sent as a guide from beyond."
~ Rumi

Your Mental Life:

- ◊ Being more aware of your own needs
- ◊ Becoming more honest with yourself
- ◊ Being more conscious to speak your own truth
- ◊ Learning to say 'no'
- ◊ Saying 'yes' and 'no' when appropriate
- ◊ Remembering you are more than just your mind
- ◊ Remembering the mind and ego are ruled by fear
- ◊ Using the breath to quiet the ramblings of the mind
- ◊ Practicing your version of meditation on a regular basis
- ◊ Setting clear intentions for your day and life
- ◊ Taking actions to reduce stress
- ◊ Consciously choosing to take deep breaths to realign the body when stressed
- ◊ Being conscious of your money flow
- ◊ Making sure your income is more than your spending
- ◊ Save on a regular basis
- ◊ Paying off debts on a regular basis
- ◊ Bookending the day with gratitude
- ◊ Acknowledging and honoring all your accomplishments

Choose action over apathy.
Wisdom over desperation.
Generosity over greed.
An apology over being right.
Remember any action will eventually become a memory.

Your Emotional Life:

- ◊ Prioritizing your relationship with yourself first
- ◊ Remembering you have needs
- ◊ Acknowledging your needs
- ◊ Honoring your needs
- ◊ Balancing the Feminine, Masculine and Child through The Council
- ◊ Being grateful to all aspects of your being
- ◊ Being conscious to embody your Feminine Power
- ◊ Loving yourself exquisitely
- ◊ When you forget to love yourself exquisitely, celebrate when you remember!
- ◊ Acknowledging all that you have already accomplished
- ◊ Letting go of caring so much about what others think of you or your actions
- ◊ Releasing the concern whether people like you or not
- ◊ Lovingly eliminating negative or draining people or situations from your life
- ◊ Being honest about your feelings to yourself and others
- ◊ Accepting and honoring your shadow side, the bitch and all
- ◊ Expressing your anger in a healthy and positive way
- ◊ Being loving and compassionate to yourself, even when you make mistakes
- ◊ Asking for what you need when you are upset
- ◊ When overly emotional, remembering to breathe
- ◊ Expressing your truth as a sensual and sexual being
- ◊ Finding space to express your deepest desires

Your Spiritual Life:

- Living in faith and love rather than fear
- Continuing to forgive yourself and others
- Being kind and loving to yourself as well as others
- Giving and receiving acts of kindness daily
- Being of service to yourself first
- Once full to overflowing, being of service to others
- When feeling anger and resentment, eventually calling on forgiveness
- Transforming any moment into a spiritual moment
- Giving yourself the opportunity and space to play
- Eliminating some of your timelines
- Practicing stillness and silence
- Giving yourself space to just be
- Embodying creative practices, whatever they may be
- Becoming conscious of life's symbology and messages
- Personifying your Higher Self through spiritual practice
- Remembering you are a spirit living in a human body
- Knowing that by changing your breath, you are changing your mind
- Being deeply grateful for all that you have and all that you are
- Creating the life you desire
- Consciously bridging the world of the mundane with the sacred

Be the life you dream of. Become the life you desire.
Live the life you love. Love the life you live.
Love all of who you are.

Now notice in which of the four categories are you the strongest and which is your weakest link. Let go of any judgment and simply make a loving commitment to yourself to pay more attention to these areas, which may be feeling a little ignored at this moment in time.

◆ Which is your weakest link?

◆ Which is your strongest link?

◆ Write down three acts of love which will cherish and honor you:

commit fully to these acts of love as a way to build trust in yourself.

LIVE AS YOU DIE

with your honor intact.

In 'A Woman's Truth', the concept of 'living out your dash' is explored. The idea that you are born and you die, yet the little dash between these two numbers on you gravestone actually epitomizes your life. Therefore, the importance is to have no regrets and to feel you have fully lived the magnitude of this little dash called life.

Therefore, as you walk your path, it is vital that you do not sell yourself short. Whatever twists and turns you may be taking, it is important to inquire if you are still living in your integrity and honor. It is said that who you are in times of extreme stress is a strong depiction of your inherent nature. If life brought you to your knees through your survival being threatened the question is, would you steal or share?

"A while ago I did a year-long meditation called 'A Year to Live'. During this experience of thinking these were my last days alive, it brought poignancy to many aspects of my life. During one of the months, I noticed that whenever I was in a life threatening situation, such as someone trying to kill me on the road, the word that would fly out of my mouth would be a short, sharp swear word! I decided if this was to be my final moment, I did not want F**k to be my last imprint. So I decided to choose a new word, one from my Reiki healing world and practiced saying it often. It was all working well until I nearly stepped on a rattlesnake while hiking. As I leapt into the air, a mutant merging of swearing and my mantra flew out of my mouth. Well it was a start!" ~ Miranda

It seems as though each human being is born with certain qualities, strengths and weaknesses. In the final hour, it is all about choosing the qualities you want to live by. Do you invoke admiration and respect as your foothold? On the other hand, as life deals the cards, are you caving into fear, scarcity and resentment?

Imagine you have a quiver of arrows by your side. It contains every aspect of who you are, the good, the bad and the ugly. It is your choice as a grown, powerful woman to decide which arrows you want to shoot into your life.

write down some of your noble attributes that support you in standing strong amidst the chaos of the storm?

TO BE

we are human beings, not human doings.

What would happen if you allowed yourself no agenda, no timeline, no have to's, no should's and you gave up caring what other people thought of you. This would truly be liberation and freedom. Imagine in any moment, choosing to be authentic to your truth, your calling, and your inner guidance. From this place of resolve, you could lovingly allow others to have their opinions, thoughts and behaviors. This would eliminate you drinking in the stress surrounding what they 'should do' which can become like a toxic poison. Instead, you can internally smile and let the judgment in your own head and those of others, no longer contaminate you. When you are standing strong in your own shaft of light, other people's opinions will not stain the love or adoration of yourself. This really would be a beautiful life for you to live in.

CHOOSE WHAT MAKES YOUR HEART SING:

- ◊ **Being Thankful**
- ◊ **Being Playful**
- ◊ **Being Original**
- ◊ **Being Spontaneous**
- ◊ **Being Young**
- ◊ **Being Bold**
- ◊ **Being Messy**
- ◊ **Being Authentic**
- ◊ **Being Mysterious**
- ◊ **Being Focused**
- ◊ **Being Tender**
- ◊ **Being Crazy**
- ◊ **Being Quiet**
- ◊ **Being Loud**
- ◊ **Being Sexy**
- ◊ **Being Adorable**
- ◊ **Being Wise**
- ◊ **Being Unique**
- ◊ **Being Beautiful**
- ◊ **Being Adventurous**
- ◊ **Being Vulnerable**
- ◊ **Being Unstoppable**
- ◊ **Being Daring**
- ◊ **Being Random**
- ◊ **Being Wild**
- ◊ **Being Obnoxious**
- ◊ **Being Devoted**
- ◊ **Being Unpredictable**
- ◊ **Being Free**
- ◊ **Being Brilliant**
- ◊ **Being Still**
- ◊ **Being Yourself**
- ◊ **Or Just Being...**

THE FINAL DESTINATION

where are you on this road called life?

Ultimately, there really is no final destination, unless you count death. The question is, do you really want this to be the ending point you are praying for? When you are immersed in your human experience, it is probably accurate to say that death is the one finality you are trying to dodge like a bullet and cheat as much as possible. The good news is when you combine your spiritual presence with your human presence; the charge of death no longer holds such a punch. This begs the question:

If you are instinctively repelling death, are you fully embracing life?

The following inquiry will guide you in encapsulating all that you have received and owned during this journey of 'A Woman's Truth'. Be fiercely honest as you reveal any lies you might still be living by. Emancipate yourself by clarifying your innate truths and discerning how to live the life you desire. Set the intention to unveil all known and unknown limiting beliefs, patterns and behaviors that stand in the way of you being the glorious woman that you already are.

◆ **What fills you to overflowing?**

◆ **Write down a list of habits, patterns or activities that replenish you.**
These choices will invite in qualities such as peace, happiness, compassion, patience, creativity, an open heart and a sense of being deeply present.

◆ **Are you being of service to yourself first?**
In today's world, it is imperative to invite in the higher aspects of your being. Often this needs to be on a conscious level. Otherwise, you can literally be caught in the trap of survival mode, which will lead to stress and a strong belief that you are not safe. Gratitude and generosity can no longer survive or be of service to you in this fearful space. Knowing and responding to what fills and replenishes you, can provide the support you need. Then all aspects of your True Self are allowed to come forth and lead the way.

◆ How do you feel once you are full to overflowing?
It is always helpful to know the result you seek when choosing to invest your time, money or energy into yourself.

◆ Another way to ask this is: What happens to you when you have plenty of it all?
Time, money, vitality, integrity and love?

◆ Who do you become?

*"I have worshipped woman as the living embodiment
of the spirit of service and sacrifice."*
~ Gandhi

*"I too have worshiped all us women as a living embodiment of the spirit of service
and sacrifice. Yet only when married with our authentic truth, our courageous love
for our self and the wherewithal not to sacrifice when it will cause harm is the true
essence and spirit of this embodiment."* ~ Miranda

ACTIONS ARE LOUDER THAN WORDS

Enough talking.

*I*n this eleventh hour you will have gathered many a new insight about your well-being, your needs and how you choose to live your life. The brain is a brilliant toolbox for your 'to do' lists. Yet it is the actual manifestation of putting the insights into practice, which will transform your physical world.

It is fine to know you need eight hours of sleep to function at your optimum. Yet if you are still sitting like a sack of potatoes in front of the television at midnight, instead of tucked up all cozy in bed fast asleep, your actions are fading into the distance and your wisdom is worthless.

For the teachings of 'A Woman's Truth' to become ingrained and alive within you, it is vital to choose physically to act upon that which you have learned benefits you. This may be as simple as replacing regular table salt with sea salt or as heartfelt as choosing to give three acts of kindness to yourself daily. Either way it is all about translating what you now know in your head into your heart and body. From this place of love, you can powerfully manifest change through a continuous stream of loving and attentive self-care. You will put your money where your mouth is and give yourself the gift of following through in a circle of completion.

From this place, your actions will speak louder than words and you will become a living embodiment of a woman in her power, her truth and her light.

As you shine in all your glory,
you will become a radiant beacon
and a lighthouse guiding others to do the same.

CREATING A LIVING MANIFESTO

A personal declaration of intent for living a glorious life.

The word manifesto comes from the Latin to manifest.

With the knowledge that energy follows thought, this simple expression depicts how extraordinarily powerful you truly are. In any given moment of inspiration and creativity, an idea can manifest and be birthed into form. As miraculous as this seems, this extraordinary human talent literally can manifest a good night's sleep, the creation of a child or a work of art.

In this final chapter of 'A Woman's Truth', you are about to redeem yourself by receiving the most potent gift of all. As in the Bible there are Ten Commandments to abide by, you are now to embark upon a decree of your own, which will prove beyond a doubt your devout and precious love for yourself.

As you write your own personal manifesto it will become an instrument and trusted guide to live by as you embark on your own journey with the teachings of 'A Woman's Truth' for the rest of your life.

Tailor this manifesto to become:

A Bodyguard for your innocence.

A Heroine for your worthy cause.

A Sovereign Queen to rule over your kingdom.

A Goddess to oversee your human fears.

A High Priestess to reign over your spiritual essence.

A Witness to honor your humanity.

A Champion to respect your body.

An Enchantress to protect your beauty.

Devote all of who you are to the worthiest of causes. Be your authentic, magnificent and glorious self. This manifesto is an introduction to your true being. It is a daily reminder of your excellence and your highest path. It is a firm commitment to love yourself no matter what. This will be your triumph and exultation when you choose to become the most exemplary and powerful version of you. These simple words will help align, direct and further your divine purpose with Godspeed. This is your Crowning Glory.

"The mighty oak was once a little nut that stood its ground."

WRITING A PERSONAL MANIFESTO:

Define who you are meant to be and become it. Before you begin, notice the void between your highest principals and your current reality. The purpose of this manifesto is for the splendor of its intention to over-ride the daily gossip and grind playing in your head. The words need to hold such power and strength that their mere uttering will inspire you with the courage to change the way you live.

Speak for your heart and take some precious time to answer the following:

◆ What are your highest core values?

◆ What do you regret?

◆ What makes you laugh?

◆ What gives you courage?

◆ What do you feel strongly about?

◆ What intention do you have for your life?

◆ What in your life do you fiercely need to mourn?

◆ If you banish the word 'should' from your life, who would you become?

◆ Complete the following statements:

I am…

I believe…

I love…

I value…

My priorities are…

My strengths are…

My weaknesses are…

My prejudices are…

My spiritual strongholds are…

And now just begin…

- ◆ Write without interruption.
- ◆ Weave together your answers from the previous questions.
- ◆ Notice which words were repeated. These are the foundation of your manifesto.
- ◆ It may flow out in an hour or you may play with the wording for days, weeks or even years.
- ◆ Let the writing flow without reason, editing or criticism.
- ◆ Allow yourself to dream.
- ◆ Ask yourself how you want to be remembered.
- ◆ You are inventing a plan and framework for your life.
- ◆ This decree will become a compass when you are feeling lost.
- ◆ Be positive and inspirational.
- ◆ Use strong powerful language in the present tense.
- ◆ Emphasize the language as a source of motivation for you.
- ◆ Now reduce the writings to a few words, sentences or paragraphs.
- ◆ Simplify the wording to become clear, clean and concise.
- ◆ Allow the points to be concrete, vivid and direct.
- ◆ Keep playing with the wording until it feels natural and deeply aligned with your authentic purpose. Once you are complete, write out your manifesto in the following Living Manifesto page.
- ◆ Remember, it is for your eyes only.
- ◆ You will know the manifesto is viable when you hear it rather than say it.
- ◆ Read or recite your manifesto at the beginning of each and every day.
- ◆ Let it inspire you and lead the way.

when blinded by the storm, know you are never really lost as you are the beacon to your soul and will always find a way back home to your true self.

A LIVING MANIFESTO

A personal declaration of intent for living a glorious life.

REVEAL MORE TRUTH

For the rest of your life!

Thank you for your promise and dedication to yourself throughout these teachings. Remember the original energy and intention, which inspired you to commit to this journey of self-discovery and empowerment. Be aware that this inspiration is still fully alive within you. The spark will always continue to grow if you consciously choose to shed light into this voyage of self-love and self-care.

Once you have completed the rough draft of your Living Manifesto, carve out some sacred time to write the final version in the Living Manifesto page. You can also visit Miranda's website at: www.MirandaJBarrett.com/resources/living-manifesto to print out more copies for yourself.

Acknowledge how your life is all about romancing and courting yourself. This last book is not an ending, but actually a beginning for you to live abundantly and to integrate, explore and revel in all that you have discovered. It is giving yourself permission to be authentically and outrageously you, in all your glory.

Let the adventures begin!

Your 'Truth Work' is simple:

Continue taking exquisite and beautiful care of yourself, every day.

This is the mission.

The glory of living in this energy is that you will truly become the Queen of your Kingdom, the Goddess in all her power and fully crowned in the magnificence that is naturally you. From this place, all beings touched by your presence will receive the gift of who you are. It has truly been an honor, a pleasure and a joy spending this precious time with you. As I sit in the presence of your transformation and power, I know for this world to be filled with glorious women such as you, will ultimately be our saving grace.

I thank you, I commend you, I respect you, I bow to you,
I honor you. And I make one last request:

Do not forget.
Live the teachings.
Spread the word.
Become a mentor, a beacon, a guide.
Live your truth.
Embody your power.
Love yourself deeply.
And always, always remember, it is you and only you
who makes your journey of life truly worth living.

I send you my love, my light and blessings
for the glorious life, which has always awaited you,

Miranda

ABOUT MIRANDA

A spirited guide and mentor.

Miranda is a passionate and devoted leader. Her loving and wise support will guide you on a transformational journey as her powerful teachings unveil the truth of who you are. Her gift is to offer potent tools, which inspire exquisite and beautiful self-care and empower you to live the fullest and most authentic life possible. As a mentor and guide, Miranda deeply walks her talk and is fearless about her own path of self-discovery, as she weaves the sacred into the mundane.

The simple, yet powerful premise offered by the mystic Rumi is the foundation of Miranda's philosophy and mission:

> *"Never give from the depths of your well, always give from your overflow."*

Miranda gives Council and Guidance for the Mind, Body and Spirit. With a background in Nutrition and Energy work, Miranda is the Creator of 'A Woman's Truth' and 'The Spirit of Energy', an Author, a Workshop and Retreat Leader, a Reiki Master and Yoga and Meditation teacher. Miranda studies under the guidance of her Beloved teachers Rod Stryker and Adyashanti.

To speak with or follow Miranda, please call or visit:

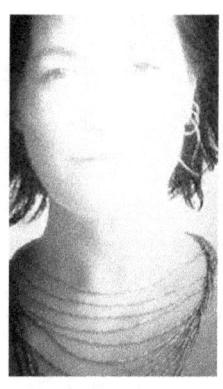

Phone: 626~798~6544
eMail: Info@MirandaJBarrett.com
Website: www.MirandaJBarrett.com
Facebook: Miranda J Barrett
Twitter: MirandaJBarrett

ABOUT HELENA

A visionary artist.

Helena Nelson-Reed is a visionary artist whose primary medium is watercolor. Born in Seattle, Washington, she was raised in Marin County and Napa Valley, California and today lives in Illinois. A largely self-taught artist whose educational emphasis and degree is in psychology, Nelson-Reed's primary focus is exploring the collective consciousness and the portrayal of archetypal imagery in the tradition of Carl Jung and Joseph Campbell. Rendered in luminous watercolor technique often described as ephemeral, Nelson-Reed's paintings are created in extraordinary detail, pushing the medium of watercolor past the usual limits. Her work may be found in private collections, book covers, magazines and cd covers. Nelson-Reed also has a line of jewelry, calendars and greeting cards.

Helena's Mission:

My images can be interpreted many ways, and for some will serve as portal to the mythic landscape. Descriptions providing background about each painting are available by request. Navigating and translating myth into contemporary wisdom is the traditional way of transmitting information though a shamanic and multi-cultural practice.

Myth, fairy, folk and spiritual lore describe divine beings and supernatural life forms arriving unbidden and disguised. In our earthly dimension, mortals often play similar roles in the lives of one another. Destinies and energies collide and interact, visible and invisible forces are at work. The mythic realms are timeless, offering insight and inspiration. While my paintings have a positive energy, many have roots in the shadows of life experience and human psyche; like the lotus blossom rooted in pond mud. For many, life is one challenge followed by the next, like beads on an endless string.

Take heart! Like goddess Inanna, one may navigate the underworld, move through dark places yet return to the realms of light battle scarred but wiser, richer for the experience. Read the ancient tales, the great mythic literature; draw strength, for they are repositories of wisdom.

Visit Helena's website for her art, purchase information and art to wear jewelry:

eMail: HNelsonReed@Gmail.com
Websites: www.HelenaNelsonReed.com
www.etsy.com/shop/HelenaNelsonReed
Blog: www.dancingdovestudio.blogspot.com
Facebook: MorningDove Design By Helena

MIRANDA'S WORLD

*Ways to stay connected
and aligned with your truth.*

BOOKS:

A Woman's Truth
A life truly worth living.

Priceless teachings reveal your transformational
journey ahead. Obstacles to self-care are explored
as clear and loving intentions are conceived.

The Grandeur Of Sleep
Permission to rest.

Miraculous benefits are realized as the worlds of sleep,
relaxation and rejuvenation are explored and deeply honored.

Nourishing Nutrition
Reclaim your health and vitality.

Reap the bountiful rewards while eating as nature intended.
Claim your health and vitality with these simple,
yet powerful tools to nourish and heal your body.

Embodying Movement
Ground your whole being.

Restore balance in your life. Discover how to embrace
your whole being through the life-enhancing benefits of body movement.

Body Care
Cherish your body as a temple.

Learn to honor your extraordinary body
as a living temple and listen to the healing messages she whispers.

Feminine Power
Fully access your supreme birthright.

Welcome and reclaim this intrinsic privilege while living
in harmonious balance between the masculine and the feminine.

The Abundance Of Wealth
Receive the gifts of prosperity.

Understand the energy flow of prosperity and weave
the threads of abundance throughout the tapestry of your life.

Find Your Authentic Voice
The courage to express who you truly are.

Your greatest ally is born
when you courageously speak your truth and claim your unique power.

Loving Yourself
A love affair with the self.

As you become highly attuned to your own needs,
allow love to lead the way. Grant yourself permission
to honor and express your heart's truest desires.
Love yourself, no matter what.

Living A Spiritual Life
Ground your divine essence here on earth.

Discover what spirituality means to you, by consciously
living between the two worlds of the sacred and the mundane.

Service As A Way of Life
Ignite the fire of love to truly be of service.

By utilizing the gems of exquisite self-care
on a daily basis and honoring your truth, your mission of service is born.

The Crowning Glory
Fully Rejoice in Being You.

A celebration overflowing with love,
blessings, grace and gratitude. Stand confident within
your truth as your mind begins to serve your heart.

The Food of Life
The versatile vegetable.

More than just a cookbook,
a comprehensive guide for nourishing your life.

Reiki
The Spirit of Energy.

An insightful guidebook full of wisdom
which introduces you to the potent and healing world of Reiki.

CARDS:

Inspiration Cards
A daily Spiritual Practice.

Sixty-Five cards with simple yet inspirational qualities
to live by and an insightful guidebook to lead the way.

CD'S:

The Grandeur of Sleep and Rejuvenating Rest

An ancient healing art of rest and relaxation.

Simple yet profound practices, which alleviate stress and tension allowing your mind, body and spirit to heal, restore and replenish.

TO ORDER PLEASE VISIT:

www.MirandaJBarrett.com
www.Amazon.com

All books are available in printed or eBook form.

TESTIMONIES
to 'A Woman's Truth' teachings.

"Never before have I experienced such an all-encompassing, yet provocative and revealing book series. I will never see myself in the same light again and I am forever grateful for this transformation."

Sarah ~ Consultant ~ Del Mar, CA

"The tools provided by the 'A Woman's Truth' book series have proven invaluable in navigating today's world. Each book gave me insight into aspects of being a woman that I had not considered before. Miranda has been an unbelievable resource on so many levels. I love telling other women about this amazing experience."

Susie ~ Out of The Box Design ~ Pasadena, CA

"Miranda is gifted with the ability to gently unearth and shine light on the broken, open spaces inside us yearning to be healed. I never realized my Male and Female aspects had very separate needs and were at war with each other until I took the journey of 'A Woman's Truth'. This book series provides essential tools for self-love, self-care and spiritual progress. We all have a special path to take and Miranda and her work helps to navigate this path with Grace. I am so very grateful that I was able to take read these books. As I write these words, I'm sending out a prayer for the Divine nectar of knowledge contained within 'A Woman's Truth' somehow reaches the lives of all women on the planet."

Shaun ~ Owner, Shaun Thompson PR ~ Redondo Beach, CA

www.ingramcontent.com/pod-product-compliance
Lightning Source LLC
Chambersburg PA
CBHW080525110426
42742CB00017B/3237